EDGE BOOKS™

ARCHAEOLOGICAL MYSTERIES

# SECRETS OF THE TERRACOTTA ARMY

## TOMB OF AN ANCIENT CHINESE EMPEROR

BY MICHAEL CAPEK

Consultant:
Hanchao Lu
Professor of History
Georgia Institute of Technology
Atlanta, Georgia

CAPSTONE PRESS
a capstone imprint

Edge Books are published by Capstone Press,
1710 Roe Crest Drive, North Mankato, Minnesota 56003
www.capstonepub.com

**Library of Congress Cataloging-in-Publication Data**
Capek, Michael.
Secrets of the terracotta army : tomb of an ancient Chinese emperor / by Michael
Capek.
    pages cm.—(Edge books. Archaeological mysteries)
Includes bibliographical references and index.
Summary: "Describes the archeological wonders of the Terracotta Army, including
discovery, artifacts, ancient peoples, and preservation"—Provided by publisher.
ISBN 978-1-4765-9917-5 (library binding)
ISBN 978-1-4765-9926-7 (paperback)
ISBN 978-1-4765-9922-9 (eBook pdf)
1. Qin shi huang, Emperor of China, 259 B.C.-210 B.C.—Tomb—Juvenile literature.
2. Terra-cotta sculpture, Chinese—Qin-Han dynasties, 221 B.C.-220 A.D.—Juvenile
literature. 3. Shaanxi Sheng (China)—Antiquities—Juvenile literature. 4. Excavations
(Archaeology)—China—Shaanxi Sheng—Juvenile literature. I. Title.
DS747.9.Q254C37 2015
931'.04—dc23                                                                    2014007003

**Developed and Produced by Focus Strategic Communications, Inc.**
    Adrianna Edwards: project manager
    Ron Edwards: editor
    Rob Scanlan: designer and compositor
    Karen Hunter: media researcher
    Francine Geraci: copy editor and proofreader
    Wendy Scavuzzo: fact checker

**Photo Credits**
Age fotostock: Shigeki Tanaka, 25; Alamy: National Geographic Image Collection,
23, 24; Deborah Crowle Illustrations, 4; Dreamstime: John Chemycz, 11; Landov:
Reuters/Jason Lee, 26, Reuters/Jose Miguel Gomez, 27, UPI/Stephen Shaver, 28;
National Geographic Creative: Hsien-Min Yang, 19, O. Louis Mazzatenta, 5, 7;
Newscom: Robert Harding/Tim Graham, 13, ZUMA Press/Lan Shan, 6; Shutterstock:
Bob Cheung, 22, Craig Hanson, 16, Hung Chung Chih, 8, 12, 29, Inna Felker, 21,
lapas77, 3, 8–9 (back), 9 (front), 20–21 (back), Mario Savoia, cover, 1, milosk50, 4–5
(back), 10, 14–15 (back), 26–27 (back), pcruciatti, 17, raymoe81, 15

Design Elements by Shutterstock

# TABLE OF CONTENTS

CHAPTER 1   A BURIED ARMY EMERGES ..................... 4

CHAPTER 2   REBUILDING AN ARMY ........................ 8

CHAPTER 3   AN ARMY FOR AN EMPEROR ............... 14

CHAPTER 4   THE END OF QIN ............................... 20

CHAPTER 5   SAVING THE ANCIENT ARMY ............... 26


GLOSSARY ..................................................... 30

READ MORE .................................................... 31

CRITICAL THINKING USING THE COMMON CORE .... 31

INTERNET SITES .............................................. 32

INDEX ........................................................... 32

# CHAPTER ONE

# A BURIED ARMY EMERGES

Farmers digging in the dark pit were frightened. For centuries they had heard about evil spirits that lurked beneath the soil in this field. Strange things had been seen here. Faces were said to have loomed suddenly out of the dirt when people had dug too deeply. Grasping hands had sometimes appeared. People had long whispered about these ghosts. Some thought they might be the guardians of the ancient emperor, whose tomb was nearby. Maybe it was the long-dead emperor himself!

## LOCATION OF TERRACOTTA ARMY

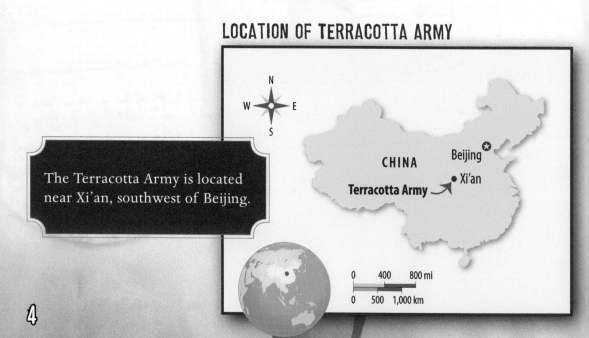

The Terracotta Army is located near Xi'an, southwest of Beijing.

In March 1974 the farmers were digging a well near Xi'an, China. About 12 feet (3.7 meters) down, they struck something. They cleared the dirt from around the object. A face appeared! Terrified, they soon saw the face was not that of a ghost at all. It was an amazingly real-looking **terracotta** head. They dug deeper and found other large pieces of hard baked clay. These appeared to be the broken parts of an ancient warrior statue.

The farmers were excited. This discovery was too important to keep secret!

terracotta—a brown-orange clay

Workers gradually uncovered terracotta figures.

## AN UNDERGROUND ARMY

Word of the amazing discovery spread fast. Soon **archaeologists** from all over China began to arrive. They were excited to see the terracotta pieces the farmers had found. The statue pieces were different from anything found in China before. The head appeared to be of an ancient warrior. Tests showed that the terracotta was more than 2,000 years old. The clay pieces had once been brightly painted, but the color faded quickly once exposed to light and air.

archaeologist—a scientist who studies how people lived in the past by analyzing their artifacts

Archaeologists unearth more terracotta warriors in 2009. Like during past excavations, they needed to be very careful not to damage the statues.

The archaeologists wondered if there might be more statues buried in the field. They dug many test holes in the ground. Nearly every place they looked had more statues and broken bits of terracotta. The buried statues were those of warriors in full battle gear. The archaeologists also found pieces of real weapons—swords, arrows, spears, and **crossbows**.

After months of careful digging, they found thousands of life-size warrior statues buried in the field. But who could have made this incredible army—and why?

# CROSSBOWS

Crossbows have been used as weapons in hunting and warfare for thousands of years. The first crossbows were invented in China about 400 BC, and possibly as early as 2000 BC. Crossbows are smaller and easier to use than bows and arrows. Crossbows spread throughout the world and changed the way people fought wars.

crossbow—a weapon based on the bow and arrow

# CHAPTER TWO

# REBUILDING AN ARMY

Months passed, and the dig grew wider and deeper. Searchers found **artifacts** in four pits. The pits had once been rooms in a building buried under 6 feet (1.8 m) of soil. The floors of the pits had been paved with bricks. Beneath the bricks were pipes to drain away any water that entered the rooms.

There were thousands of warrior statues standing in the pits. The workers also discovered pieces of terracotta horses and **chariots**.

Archaeologists have pieced together a bronze chariot from fragments.

But the number of warrior statues surprised the workers most. The warriors seemed to be everywhere. Nearly all of them were broken into small pieces. It took archaeologists and trained workers many months just to put one statue back together. Each ruined warrior had to be rebuilt by hand, like a huge jigsaw puzzle.

artifact—an object used in the past that was made by people

chariot—a light, two-wheeled cart pulled by horses

## PIECES OF A PUZZLE

About 2,000 Terracotta warriors have been reassembled. The rest are still in pieces or lie buried. Experts think about 8,000 Terracotta warriors may have once stood in the pits.

## WARRIORS OF ALL KINDS

Even before the warriors were put back together, researchers could tell that each one looked different. Some seemed older than others. Eyes and noses were different shapes. Each statue had its own hairstyle. There were many varieties of clothes and shoes on the warriors. Some smiled, while others seemed angry. Some had mustaches and beards. Others looked too young to have facial hair at all. Their sizes and poses were all slightly different as well.

Terracotta warriors

There were several kinds of warriors. The clothing and weapons on the statues showed what role each soldier played in the army. Statues of many common soldiers wore **tunics** and carried swords and shields. Some wore **fishscale armor**, which helped protect ancient Chinese warriors in battle. Warrior statues with longer beards were placed behind the ranks of soldiers. These statues were of older warriors, maybe officers. Most of the soldiers were standing, but some were kneeling. Many of the kneeling statues were archers designed to hold real bows and arrows or crossbows.

tunic—a long, loose-fitting shirt

fishscale armor—a kind of armor worn in ancient times made up of overlapping plates that looked like the scales of a fish

Most of the Terracotta Army figures held actual weapons. The weapons were not made of terracotta. They slowly fell apart after being exposed to moisture in the ground.

## MORE MYSTERIES IN THE PITS

Years passed and the archaeologists kept digging. The search area stretched out across the field for more than 1 mile (1.6 kilometers). Everywhere they dug, they found more and more statues. One of the pits had statues of the army's highest officers. Their clothing was fancier, and these statues were taller than most of the others. Together a team of scientists searched for answers about the warriors buried in the pits.

Terracotta Army officer

# MOLDS

Scientists have learned that all of the warrior statues were made from molds. Wet clay was put into wooden forms to make parts of the warriors' bodies—arms, legs, and heads. Then skilled artists took the clay out of the molds and added certain details to each piece. This was done by hand. The artists wanted to make each warrior different. All of the parts were then fired in **kilns**. The artists applied a special coating that sealed the terracotta pieces together into a solid statue. The final step was to paint the statues with bright colors.

kiln—a hot oven used to fire clay

Like the original builders of the Terracotta Army, historians today also use molds to make copies of the soldiers. These replicas are sometimes displayed in museums.

# CHAPTER THREE

# AN ARMY FOR AN EMPEROR

Over time the team of experts began to find answers about the terracotta figures. Old Chinese histories spoke of the burial of Qin Shi Huangdi (CHIN SHIH huang-DEE), the first emperor of China.

The emperor was one of the richest and most powerful rulers who ever lived. He ruled China more than 2,000 years ago. His army was one of the most feared in the world. None of the emperor's many enemies dared attack while his army was on alert. But ancient books said that Qin Shi Huangdi feared his own death. He wanted to have his army to protect him in the next life.

While he was still young, the emperor gave orders to build a vast underground tomb for himself. The workers were also told to make a perfect model of his whole kingdom.

Inside he wanted a model of everything he loved in order to live in comfort and safety in the next life. People in ancient China believed that objects buried with them would make them comfortable in the afterlife.

# QIN SHI HUANGDI

Qin Shi Huangdi, the first emperor of China, was also known as Ying Zheng. He was only 13 when he became king of the state of Qin. At age 22 he led his army to victory over nine other states. His royal name, Qin Shi Huangdi, means "the first emperor of the Qin Dynasty."

statue of Qin Shi Huangdi

Terracotta horses and grooms

## A CITY FOR SPIRITS

The emperor's army was the most important thing in the world to him during his life. Without it his many enemies would have attacked and taken away everything he had. Scientists agree that the Terracotta Army was Qin's way of taking his army with him after death.

There were also other things buried in the pits that the emperor valued. One was a huge garden. It had a park surrounded by many beautiful clay birds and animals. It even included a clay boatman and a real boat for the emperor to ride in. There was a stable with horses and **grooms**. Scientists also found a foundation of a grand palace. The emperor's whole tomb was meant to be a huge city. There he could live in luxury, just as he had while he was alive.

groom—a person who cleans, brushes, and cares for horses

After years of searching, archaeologists have discovered that the emperor's entire tomb covered more than 30 square miles (78 square kilometers). It included nearly 60 separate underground sections, including the Terracotta Army. Experts now see that all of the sections were part of Qin's master plan. He achieved the full-size underground "spirit city" he wanted.

**ARCHAEOLOGICAL FACT**

Historians say that more than 700,000 people worked on Qin's tomb while he was alive. The tomb was constructed between 228 and 246 BC. Many of the emperor's servants were killed at the time of his death so they could make the emperor comfortable in the next world.

Archaeologists excavate near Qin's tomb.

## SKILLED WORKERS

Archaeologists have found skeletons of workers who built the tomb. They found that many workers had suffered broken bones and wounds. Often these injuries had been carefully treated as if by a skilled doctor. Tests done on bones and tooth enamel also showed many of the workers were well fed and healthy. The well-treated workers may have been artists or had special skills. Their creative work was probably seen as important. They had to be kept healthy if the tomb was ever to be finished.

Many thousands of workers created Qin's tomb.

**ARCHAEOLOGICAL FACT**

Nearly all the terracotta pieces have names carved into them. Experts believe the names are of the makers of the terracotta statues. These include both men's and women's names.

Many graves have been found near the pits. Some of the graves contain the bones of people killed in horrible ways. Historians believe these workers may have been killed to keep them from telling exactly where the emperor's spirit city was located. Some clearly were prisoners—chains and even clay tablets listing their crimes were found buried with them.

# CHAPTER FOUR

# THE END OF QIN

Records show that Emperor Qin Shi Huangdi died in 210 BC at the age of 50. As Qin had expected, China exploded into warfare immediately after his death. Hoping to take power for themselves, enemies attacked Qin's capital city. They killed his family and anyone loyal to him. They burned Qin's fine homes and palaces. Then they turned their anger on the parts of the emperor's tomb they could find.

Rebels dug tunnels to get into the underground chambers where the Terracotta Army stood guard. The looters stole many of the weapons.

## ARCHAEOLOGICAL FACT

To warriors of ancient China, weapons as fine as those made for the emperor's army were more valuable than gold.

# METAL WEAPONS

Artifacts found in the pits show how advanced the ancient Chinese were in making metal weapons. They knew the secret to making hard, strong metal weapons that would not break during heavy fighting. Modern science did not rediscover this secret until many centuries later.

Metal weapons on the Great Wall of China display the metalworking skills of the ancient Chinese.

## LOOTING DAMAGE

It appears the rebels broke many of the Terracotta warriors. They also set fire to the wooden structure that had housed the soldiers. It fell, burning and crushing the figures, chariots, and other items inside. Chinese history books record this fire. It lasted for three months. Archaeologists figured out what had happened from clues they found as they dug. Tests of soil showed that the pits were full of charred wood. Also, many clay bricks and terracotta pieces were a dark red color and badly cracked. This damage could only have been caused by a very hot fire. Putting the evidence together, archaeologists came to understand what must have happened to the Terracotta Army.

burned and broken terracotta pieces caused by looters

## The Army Is Reburied

Evidence shows that in the years following the attack on the emperor's tomb, the site changed. The ruined underground building and shattered army were slowly reburied when floods from the nearby Wei River brought silt and mud. Centuries of rain and wind laid down more dirt and dust. After 1,000 years no sign of the pits could be seen.

New rulers of China came and went, but the area where Qin made his burial grounds was left alone. After hundreds of years, people forgot about Qin and his magnificent army. Stories were told of the First Emperor's magnificent tomb complex, but not of the buried army. The world forgot that the warriors were there.

The area where Emperor Qin was buried is now heavily covered with trees and grass.

## DON'T WAKE THE EMPEROR

The mound where the emperor was buried has changed too. At one time it was a step-pyramid. Earth was piled up and packed down in step-shapes. The hill was 394 feet (120 m) high. A chamber deep beneath the hill held the body of Qin and the treasures buried with him. Today the hill is smaller. **Erosion** has left it at a height of 210 feet (64 m).

erosion—the wearing away of land by water or wind

Emperor Qin is buried under a hill (foreground) that remains untouched.

There were many stories of rich treasure inside the tomb. But historians believe that no one ever disturbed the mound. One reason may be that the Chinese people have always honored the spirits of ancestors. Some people feared they would be haunted by ancient ghosts. Others simply respected the memory of the dead. Today most Chinese leaders think that great rulers, even those who were cruel and selfish, should be left in peace.

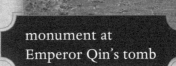

monument at
Emperor Qin's tomb

# CHAPTER FIVE

# SAVING THE ANCIENT ARMY

Research and digging continue on the Terracotta Army. Archaeologists are constantly making new discoveries. They believe many more amazing artifacts still lie buried, waiting to be discovered. But they have to be careful. They know that silk, wood, pottery, or paper buried deep underground will crumble once exposed to light and air. The emperor's tomb is nearby. But until science can find a way to safely explore the wonders of the tomb, it will have to remain sealed.

Technicians carefully restore a Terracotta Army statue in June 2010.

# USING TECHNOLOGY INSTEAD OF DIGGING

Scientists are now using technology to see what is underground. A device sends sound waves deep into the earth. When the sound waves strike a hard object, they bounce back. They can be read by a computer and turned into an image. Scientists can create a picture of the entire underground site without having to dig!

technology device used for "seeing" underground

# A Home for the Warriors

Millions of people visit the Terracotta Army every year at the Terracotta Warriors and Horses Museum near Xi'an, China. Visitors can walk around the pits and see the restored warriors. They can watch archaeologists at work restoring and studying the ancient figures.

The museum is also home to a library and exhibit halls. People from all over the world come to see many of the artifacts that have been found with the soldiers. Museum guides give demonstrations and explain how items were found and what they reveal about the past. Careful research by archaeologists and other scientists will preserve the Terracotta Army artifacts for future generations.

interior of Terracotta Warriors and Horses Museum

# New Enemies Threaten

Great steps have been taken to protect the Terracotta Army for the future. But recent studies show that the warriors may be in serious danger. Scientists have learned that a better system of air control is needed at the museum. Pollutants such as mold and dust along with heat in the museum are causing the clay warriors to crack and break down. The air in the museum must be kept at a steady temperature and humidity level. It must also be filtered to remove harmful particles too small to see.

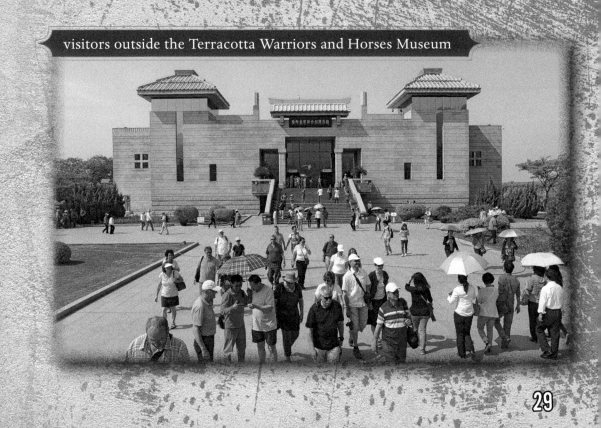
visitors outside the Terracotta Warriors and Horses Museum

# GLOSSARY

**archaeologist** (ar-kee-AH-luh-jist)—a scientist who studies how people lived in the past by analyzing their artifacts

**artifact** (AR-tuh-fact)—an object used in the past that was made by people

**chariot** (CHAYR-ee-uht)—a light, two-wheeled cart pulled by horses

**crossbow** (KRAWS-boh)—a weapon based on the bow and arrow

**erosion** (i-ROH-zhuhn)—the wearing away of land by water or wind

**fishscale armor** (FISH-skale AR-muhr)—a kind of armor worn in ancient times made up of overlapping plates that looked like the scales of a fish

**groom** (GROOM)—a person who cleans, brushes, and cares for horses

**kiln** (KILN)—a hot oven used to fire clay

**terracotta** (ter-uh-KOT-uh)—a brown-orange clay

**tunic** (TOO-nik)—a long, loose-fitting shirt

# READ MORE

**Cohen, Jessica.** *The Ancient Chinese.* Crafts from the Past. New York: Gareth Stevens, 2013.

**Malam, John.** *Terracotta Army and Other Lost Treasures.* Lost and Found. Irvine, Cal.: QEB Publishing, 2011.

**Pilegard, Virginia Walton.** *The Emperor's Army.* Gretna, La.: Pelican Publishing Company, 2010.

**Roberts, Russell.** *Ancient China.* Explore Ancient Worlds. Hockessin, Del.: Mitchell Lane, 2013.

# CRITICAL THINKING
# USING THE COMMON CORE

1. Using text from page 25, list at least three reasons why Emperor Qin's burial ground may have been left alone. Which reason do you think probably played the biggest role, and why? (Key Ideas and Details)

2. Find three examples in the book of what an archaeologist does. What do you think the advantages and disadvantages of working as an archaeologist would be? (Key Ideas and Details)

3. On page 18, the author suggests that the workers who appear to have been well cared for may have been artists or had special skills. What reasons does the author give to support this statement? Do you agree? Why or why not? (Integration of Knowledge and Ideas)

## INTERNET SITES

FactHound offers a safe, fun way to find Internet sites related to this book. All of the sites on FactHound have been researched by our staff.

Here's all you do:

Visit *www.facthound.com*

Type in this code: 9781476599175

Check out projects, games, and lots more at
www.capstonekids.com

## INDEX

archaeologists, 6, 7, 8, 9, 12, 17, 18, 22, 26, 27, 28
armor, 11
artifacts, 8, 21, 26, 28

chariots, 8, 22
clothing, 10, 11, 12
crossbows, 7, 11, 25

horses, 8, 16

looting, 20, 22

metal, 21

paint, 6, 13
pits, 8, 9, 12, 16, 19, 21, 22, 23, 28

Qin Shi Huangdi, 14, 15, 16, 17, 18, 20, 23, 24, 25
 burial mound of, 24, 25
 tomb preservation of, 28–29

reassembly of statues, 9, 13, 28

Terracotta Warriors and Horses Museum, 28, 29

weapons, 7, 11, 20, 21
workers (on Qin's tomb), 18, 19

Xi'an, China, 4, 5, 28

Ying Zheng, 15